TRUE LOVE'S REVELATION

A Collection of Poems

Demetria S. Patton

Dear Reader:

Thank you for taking time, you will never get back, to read my work. I am immensely honored and appreciative.

It's from a place of revelation that the poems you will read on the following pages were written. They are poems about Him: the Lover of my soul and the King of my heart. They are poems about His creation: the ones He sent His only, begotten Son Jesus Christ to save. They are poems about me: a sinner saved by grace who can now be called a child of the Most High God because of Jesus's life, death, burial, resurrection, and ascension.

It is my sincerest hope that this collection inspires you to develop a relationship with God so you too can receive the revelations He has for you and your life!

With love,
Demetria S. Patton

CONTENTS

REVELATION OF HIM

L.O.V.E.

LOVE is everything My Word proclaimed it to be centuries upon centuries ago. It has not changed because I do not change. It is not as elusive as the enemy of your soul wants you to believe. It is easily found and freely given because I am Love.

Oh, but that's right. You do not want Love because you do not want Me. You have turned your face from Me and declared in your heart that I will not be your God.

Verily surely I tell you, I will not force you to choose Me— to choose Love. As much as it grieves Me, I will continue to allow you to cast your eyes out into the world and choose Love's counterfeit.

Everyone who has ears let them hear. I am what your hearts are longing for. My absence is why your souls are crying out. Choose Me. I am subject to no one. No one is like Me, and no one can arraign Me. There were no gods formed before Me or after Me. I know no other gods. For I am the one, true living God. I drive out and overcome the darkness. I invade and reign. I do not lead you out like a wolf in sheep's clothing to be devoured. I keep truth forever. I protect. I do not numb your pain by ministering death. I heal and give life. I do not condemn or hold your sins against you. I forgive, restore, and return to you that which was lost. I do not give you rest that can be induced by a pill in a bottle. No, I give true rest and with Me your sleep will be sweet. I do not give peace as the world gives. The peace I give passes all understanding. My creation, hear the truth laid bare: I sent My only, begotten Son to die on the cross for your sins. I love you. For that is who I am. Choose Me. Choose Love.

<u>CHOOSE LOVE</u>

When did My name become a byword?
A curse on the tongue of My creation,
The ones I created in My image,
The ones I sent My only, begotten Son to save.
I would tell you that I love you,
So that you would turn away from your destruction,
The sin that pulls you to the grave.
But I know even that perfect declaration
Would be of little consequence.
Because you don't know Me;
Therefore, you don't know Love.
This world has seared your conscience.
The enemy has distorted your perception of Love.
He has served you Love's counterfeit,
And you have consumed to the full
Its pain,
Its conditional promises,
Its bondage,
Its destruction.
So, when I proclaim that I love you,
You scoff,
You run,
Juxtaposing Love's counterfeit,
To My Love.

Because you can't begin to fathom,
That I exist,
That I created you,
For Myself.
And the only thing I want to do is love you,
Give Myself to you continually,
In revelation.
So you know who I am,
That I'm not an angry, vengeful God
But the one, true living God
Who loves you
Who knew you
Before you were formed in your mother's womb.
Who created you in eternity,
And spoke you into time.
Who covered you in your mother's womb,
Singing praises over you,
Declaring that you would be Mine.
I carved out a spot in you,
That only I could fill.
So when you were birthed into time,
You would be compelled to yield,
And find Me,
And I, true Love,
Would enter in and fill.
But woe to My creation,
You have lost your way.
You have attempted to fill My spot,
With things I didn't ordain.
That's why you are never content,
And satisfied for only a time.
Because that spot rejects Love's counterfeit,
It cannot dwell in the spot,

Meant only for God.
So now that you know,
That it's Me that you need.
Reject Love's counterfeit,
And come after Me.
Search and you will find.
Ask and you will receive.
I will enter in,
And fill the space,
I created just for Me.
In that day, I will heal and restore,
Every broken place.
I will reveal every deception,
And correct every lie.
So you will know true Love.
You will know the living God.

SEARCH AND SEE

O Child, how they search for Me,
Because the void inside,
Has their hearts longing,
And their souls crying out.

O Child, why can't they see,
I'm the only One who can fill it?
Instead of substituting Me,
For the things that kill them.

O Child, how they search for Me,
In lovers I didn't join or ordain.
In the bottom of bottles,
Attempting to fill My place.

O Child, why can't they see,
That nature proclaims my existence?
The trees, the moon, the stars,
Give testimony of My preeminence.

O Child, how they search for Me,
While desecrating the place I'm supposed to reign.
The Temple within,
Discarded and treated with disdain.

O Child, why can't they see,

I cannot be found in the world?
I am the one, true living God,
Eager to be seen and heard.

O Child, how they search for Me,
When I give of Myself freely.
I stand at the door of their hearts—knocking,
Waiting to gain entry.

O Child, why can't they see,
All they have to do is say *yes?*
And I will fill the caverns of their souls,
Giving them life, love, peace, and rest.

O Child, can you tell them,
How much they are loved?
Tell them I'm not an evil taskmaster,
Wanting to destroy them from above.

O Child, can you tell them,
That You are the Savior of the world?
Jesus Christ—their God,
Who will lead them back Home.

THE RESTRAINT TO ALLOW YOU TO CHOOSE

I urn to set you free,
From the sin that so easily ensnares you,
From death that has its grip on you,
But you won't let Me.
How much restraint it takes,
To see you bound,
Afraid,
Tossed to and fro,
By the waves,
And you continually slap,
My hand away.
You forbear My name,
You disdain My blessing,
When all I want to do is help you.
How much restraint it takes,
To hear your prayers,
And answer them.
But you still don't receive,
Because you don't receive by faith.
How much restraint it takes,
To have your prayers reach heaven's gate,

But your partnership with the enemy,
Allows him to steal your answered prayers away.
How much restraint it takes,
To be the God of abundance,
And see you beg bread,
And lack every good thing,
When I urn to supply every need.
How much restraint it takes,
To love you, My creation,
Without overriding your free will,
To give you a glimpse,
A taste,
Of the life you can have,
If you choose Me,
And My way.
How much restraint it takes,
To watch the enemy,
Lead you away as slaves,
To your death and destruction,
When it was never meant to be that way.
O My creation,
I urn,
I beg,
I plead.
With your gift of free will,
Choose Me.

SOMETHING

A travesty has occurred in the world today,
My name is not being used in the appropriate way.
My name is being ascribed to things I didn't orchestrate.
Don't you know, it's blasphemous what you say?
"Something told me to do this,
Something told me to do that."
Can I be the one to tell you,
I didn't tell you that!
It is the Holy Spirit.
The One sent by God.
To go with you,
Wherever you go.
To be with you,
Wherever you are.
The Helper, the Teacher, the Comforter.
It is He who warns you,
To keep you from harm.
It is He who nudges you,
In the right direction.
It is He who teaches you,
The Word of God.
So please stop,
Ascribing to me,
The works of the Holy One.

I am merely a word,
Used to describe something,
Unspecified and unknown.
The Holy Spirit is not unrevealed,
And now you have been warned.
The next time you receive,
A gift from above,
Give credit where credit is due,
To the Holy Spirit,
The One sent by God.

#Not "Something"

THE COMMISSION

Do you know there are people,
Designed to hear My voice through you?
Do you know that you,
Have been designed to move?
Do you know that you,
Are not meant to be stagnate?
Stuck in your sin,
Bound by the enemy,
Unable to win.
Do you know that you are free?
That I have the keys,
To unlock every mystery.
Freely I have given,
Freely I want you to receive.
Arise from the shackles,
That bind thee.
Take this key,
Set thyself free,
And come after Me.
I will reveal every mystery.
I will tell you,
Who I designed you to be.
I will show you your territory.
I will show you My sheep,

The ones you are meant to shepherd,
And set free.
I will show you their blood,
Flowing through the hills and valleys.
Arise and see,
That time is not free.
You can no longer run,
From who I've designed you to be.

MY CHURCH

Why have You forsaken Me?
You have turned against your first Love,
And gone after your own way.
Do you know that I am a jealous God?
That I share my glory with no man.
You ask me,
How have we forsaken You?
It's because you have forsaken those that I love,
The lost,
The hurt,
The destitute.
The ones who come to you,
Needing to know the truth,
Of the salvation I have for them.
And you turn your nose up,
You cast them out.
You ridicule them,
Because they can't wear the mask that you wear.
The façades they can't put on and take off,
At their leisure.
No, they come to you not having,
Learned the mechanics you have.
They come in needing,
The truth of My Word.

And you don't give it to them,
You don't help them.
How then can you call yourselves My Church?
My disciples,
My people,
The ones I have saved.
What are you doing with your salvation?
The gifts that you ask Me for and I give.
The anointing you beg Me for and I give.
What is it for?
Who is it for?
Is it for My people?
Or is it for you?
To tickle ears,
To massage egos,
To further condemn those,
Who do not look like you.
Stop!
Turn back to Me,
Your first Love,
Your true Love.
And be My disciples,
Speak My words.
Be My hands,
Be My feet,
Be My mouth,
In a dark and desolate world.
Save My people,
Be the Church that I have commanded you to be.
Because if you don't,
I will stretch out My hand,
And I will remove you from,
The seats that you fill,

And the pulpits that you speak from.
I will cast you out,
And you will no longer,
Speak My words,
Or harm My people,
From your neglect.

<u>ARISE</u>

The end is near,
My dear Church,
And you are not ready.
Asleep you are,
Lost in slumber,
And your comfort.
Where are you in this world?
Where is your light?
Where is your flavor?
My salt,
My city on a hill,
The lost can't find you.
The needy can't penetrate you.
You forbear them to enter in your walls,
To receive,
The gift I have given them.
The gift that I have freely given you.
What are you doing?
Why are you not awake?
Why can't you see the ones I love perishing?
Why are you not in an urgent state?
To save those who are lost,
Like I saved you.
Your salvation is not just for you,

To get into crowded rooms,
On Sunday mornings to fake pleasantries,
And proceed through the mechanics of salvation.
No!
You are My hands and feet.
You are My mouthpiece.
Why aren't you moving?
Why aren't you speaking?
Why are you tolerating the enemy of your soul?
Why are you letting him push you around?
Why are you letting him gain ground?
Authority you have been given,
To loose and bind,
In heaven and on earth.
Walk in the power and authority you have been given.
Rebuke the devourer,
And he will flee.
Bind his work,
Cast him out,
And he will leave.
Why are you afraid,
To do what you,
Have been commissioned to do?
Fire!
Arise!
The dawn is breaking.
It is time for your light to shine.
It is time for your gates to open.
It is time for you to arise.

PREPARE

Prepare for the great and terrible,
Day of the Lord.
My Church,
My Bride,
I am sending laborers among you,
To prepare you for My return.
Do not be deceived,
Or led astray by false doctrine.
And false prophets,
Who only want to preach the good news,
Their good news,
From the deep wells,
Of their bellies,
They prophesy lies.
To keep you in your stupor,
Comfortable and ineffective.
Unprepared for My return.
Wake up!
And take your position,
As conquerors,
As overcomers.
In these last days,
Destruction will come.
They will deliver you up,

To be killed.
Great trials and tribulations,
Will come to you for My namesake,
But you must endure to the end.
Because I will return,
To fulfill that which is written.
I will call you to Myself,
And take you Home.

<u>WATCH</u>

Don't be afraid,
As you see the world fall away.
These things must come to pass,
Because My words will be fulfilled.
In that time, I will come,
Like a thief in the night.
Surprising only the ones who aren't waiting,
But My elect will be waiting.
The anticipation of My return,
Will cause them to forbear sleep,
To ridicule it,
To disdain it.
Why should one sleep,
And miss the return of the King?
Coming to retrieve His people.
To show them,
That it has been Him all along,
The Son of the Most High God,
Calling them,
And beckoning them forward.
My precious creation,
Look toward the sky.
Do not sleep or slumber,
Or grow weary from waiting.

For I am coming soon.
Look to the sky,
From whence I came,
And returned.
I shall also come again,
To take you,
With Me,
To our Home.

RECEIVE

My return will be triumphant,
And all the world will see,
Me come on the clouds,
And fulfill what's written.
In that day, the mocker will cease,
Even they will know the truth,
And it will set them free.
Some will turn away,
From the wicked one,
And his schemes.
Some will continue,
To do his will and his deeds.
But there will come a time,
When it all will cease.
And every living, breathing creature,
Will stand before the King.
In that day, the books will be opened.
I will hear and I will judge,
The words that are spoken.
Many in that day,
Will beg and plead.
But I will not hear,
For mercy will no longer be free.
To some I will say: "Enter into My rest."

Others will hear the words,
Loud,
Thundering,
Emanating from My chest,
"Depart from Me. You will not enter into My rest."
So child as you write,
The words that you are hearing Me speak,
Warn My people,
To run after My mercy.
It is freely given in this age and time.
Tell them to take it now,
While it still can be found.

IN THE END

Be still and know that I am God.
I make My sun rise and fall,
On the righteous and the just,
On the unrighteous and the unjust.
I do not judge as man judges,
I judge rightly.
There will come a time,
When I will cease,
To push and pull you,
In the right direction.
No, I will let you choose,
Your poison.
And I will let you,
Drink to the full of your destruction.
When your death is manifesting,
You will call on Me,
And I will not answer.
For it will be too late.
Listen, while there is still time.
Find Me while I can be found.
Turn while there is still a chance.
Come back to Me,
While My arms are still open.

JUDGMENT

In a line they will stand,
One by one,
To be judged for all they have done.
In that day,
There will be nowhere to run,
Nowhere to hide,
All will have to stand,
Before the Divine.
Their lives, meticulously recorded,
Will testify their deeds.
No one will escape,
Nothing will be unseen.
All will give an account,
For what they have done,
And each will receive the judgement,
They have earned.
To some: "depart from Me."
To some: "job well done."
As it is written, the lake of fire,
Burning with brimstone,
Will swallow the deserving whole.
But to those who called,
Upon the name of the Lord,
Will be welcomed Home.

<u>COME</u>

Come and listen,
As I speak the words,
That must be written.
Warn My people,
Of the coming destruction,
That will be released,
Upon the land.
Tell them to heed My words,
Do not consider them folly.
For I speak,
And My words do not return to Me void,
No, they accomplish what I set out for them to accomplish.
Listen, My precious creation,
To the words that have been spoken.
While there is still time,
Pay attention to the signs,
Written in the skies.
Written in the cracks,
Of the world crumbling around you,
It and the pleasures of it,
Are passing away.
Can't you see,
That he will not always reign?
That the world will not always be,

Under his sway.
Turn back My children,
Turn the other way.
Turn away from your destruction,
Let My words guide the way,
Come.

REVELATION OF ME

TOGETHER

Together we are writing,
This book of poems.
So you will know that My words,
Are never wrong.
The words I give you to speak,
I want it done,
According to My will,
According to My song.
My thoughts are not your thoughts,
My ways are not your ways.
This journey requires you,
To trust me without wavering.
So we have begun here,
So I can build in you,
A trust that can't be broken,
A trust that must remain pure.

CONFESSION

O Heavenly Father,
Forgive me, for I am a sinner.
Although, intellectually I believed,
I needed a Savior.
I still believed,
Consciously and subconsciously,
In my own goodness.
Jesus said that no one was good but You.
However, I thought maybe I was the exception.
Like on a really good day I was worthy,
Of You choosing me.
I mean, it's not like I'm one of those real sinners.
The ones who break commandments,
And commit abominations.
No, far be it from me.
I don't steal…at least not in the traditional sense.
I mean I haven't always "worked" while at work,
But honestly Father, who has?
Also, I lie, but I'm not a liar.
I mean who wouldn't tell a white lie,
To get out of a ticket?
I didn't have insurance.
It's my job's fault anyway that I had to lie.
If they paid me enough, I would have insurance,

And I wouldn't have had to lie to boot.
I mean Father almost anyone in my position,
Would have done it.
Self-preservation makes man do things,
He normally wouldn't do,
And I'm no different.
Also, Father I dabble in a little deception,
But I'm not deceitful.
I mean who hasn't been busy,
Pulled in each direction,
That every "i" wasn't dotted,
And every "t" wasn't crossed,
That one had to be a little deceitful,
And throw someone else under the bus.
Again, self-preservation Father.
Also, I have idols in my life,
And I practice idolatry.
There are things that I prioritize over You.
Things I choose over You.
Things I give more of my time to than You.
Things that fill me up.
Things that help me escape.
But Father, you see the world I live in,
With its instant gratification and infinite distractions.
How can I not have idols?
Everyone has them,
You can't blame me for this,
For any of this.
Everyone does these things—and probably worse.
The world tells me they're not a big deal.
The world tells me that I'm one of the good ones.
So why are You revealing these things to me?
Why are You convicting me?

Why are You searching the hidden caverns of my soul?
Shining Your light upon my wickedness.
Why are You confronting me with my depravity?
Why are You slowly peeling back my façade?
Like a tightly secured scab.
"Because I love you.
Because I have called you.
I have set you apart,
And I am making you fit for the Master's use.
You cannot stay broken and deceived,
Tossed to and fro,
Under the sway of the world,
And the wicked one.
No, you must come out,
Into the light,
To be healed,
To be restored,
And sanctified,
Buffeted and tried.
Sent out to speak,
The words I command you to speak.
You will warn My creation,
The ones who are still under the sway,
Of the wicked one.
The ones who are still lost,
The ones who are sick,
The ones who are in need of a healer,
You will proclaim who I am to them.
You will speak My words,
Warn them of their coming destruction,
If they do not turn."

MERCIFUL AND COMPASSIONATE FATHER

O Father,
Apart from You,
I am a lost, wretched soul.
When you reveal parts of me,
That have yet to be touched by You,
I want to be no more.
I want to cease to exist.
But then I remember Your voice,
So gently in my ear,
"Return to Me child,
Even when you slip."
With my Sword in my hand,
I slay shame and guilt.
And hasten back to your throne,
To find You there with open arms.
"Why has your countenance fallen?
Why are your shoulders bowed low?
Did you forget who you are again?
A child of the King,
My chosen one.
Come now child,

And rest in My arms,
While I explain to you again,
Just Whose you are."

<u>REJECTION</u>

In my younger years,
I yearned for acceptance.
But, all I found was rejection.
My hair,
My clothes,
My personality,
I wasn't good enough,
For those around me.
Oh, how the spirit of rejection,
Dug its heels in deep.
Entrenched in my soul,
Determined to ensure my defeat.
For years it ruled,
And reigned in my life.
Influencing my decisions,
Shaping my psyche.
I compared,
I people pleased.
Accept me!
I screamed through my words, actions, and good deeds.
Rejection!
You sneaky, evil, filthy thing.
How you hid,
Robbed,

And tormented me.
But thank God,
For the Father's love.
When I was thirty-one,
He shone His light on you from above.
From Him you could not hide.
He revealed your operation in my life.
Not one,
Not two,
But three,
Prophesied,
"It's rejection!"
Casting you out,
But, you still did not flee.
It was I,
Who had to relinquish you,
From me.
So, one Sunday morning,
The Father gave me eyes to see,
You taking root in the younger me.
Growing a tree,
Anger and bitterness,
The fruit sprouting up in me.
"Confess,
Repent,
Lay it before Me,
I want to heal,
And cast it far from thee."
Obedient I was,
Through tears I spoke.
The Father heard my words,
And removed your crown.
Your reign and your trunk came tumbling down.

He snatched your stump from the ground,
Your roots attached,
No hope for a rebound.
I've been delivered.
I've been set free.
So now when you return,
Trying to plant seeds,
I stand in His power and authority.
"In the name of Jesus,"
I declare unafraid.
"I bind your works rejection,
And cast you away."

GENERATIONAL CURSES

The sins of your fathers,
Have been visited upon you.
But do not worry,
I have provided you with an escape.

Your fathers were cruel,
And refused to yield to My Word.
They were evil and hard-hearted,
Seeking their own spoils.

But you child are different,
You are not of this world.
You are My chosen vessel,
Whom I will use to speak My words.

On adventures we will go,
Up the mountains we will climb,
All the way up,
Until your face touches the sky.

There will be no limits,
To what I will do.
Your life will be a testament,
To the God you have given your life to.

The generations after you,
Will be called blessed.
Because of your honor and obedience,
They will enter into My rest.

I will shine My face upon them.
I will be there God.
I will tell of your obedience,
And the foundation their feet stands upon.

GENERATIONAL CURSES BROKEN

The iniquities of my fathers,
Caused them to leave curses as gifts.
Wrapped, stamped and already sent.
Eager for me to unveil them since I was born,
Being unaware of the contents,
I unwrapped them one by one.
Poverty,
Adultery,
Broken relationships.
Shame,
Guilt,
Rebellion,
Fear.
"Be far it from me," I said casting them out.
You devoured my fathers,
But me, you will not have,
And there is no doubt.
I am a child of the King,
And I already have the victory.
Love,
Prosperity,
Marriage,

Healing,
Obedience,
Are the only gifts I receive.
In the name of Jesus,
I decree it in heaven and on earth,
All generational curses are broken over me,
Now and forevermore.

<u>MY QUEEN</u>

Do not bow your head,
And let not your countenance fall.
Stand in the power and authority,
Of who you truly are.
You are a child of the King,
Seated in heavenly places,
With Me.
The Lamb who was slain,
The resurrected King.
In Me you have your being and identity.
Harken to,
And believe the words I speak.
So hear ye, hear ye,
The one, true King speaks,
This is My child,
In whom I am well pleased.
She is My queen,
Who will rule and reign with Me.
Because she has been faithful with little,
I will make her ruler over much,
For all of eternity.

#What He says about me

<u>MY LOVE</u>

I have known from the start,
That you were My chosen vessel.
Since before you were formed,
I called you blessed.

You were wrought in secret,
In the lowest parts of the earth.
Before your mother knew she was pregnant,
I knew you would be a girl.

The apple of My eye,
The one I would love.
The one I would give My life for,
So you could have the chance to spend eternity above.

AN ODE TO THE SAVIOR

My true Love,
How I've searched for Thee.
Even when I didn't know,
It was You I was searching for.

Your absence propelled me to look,
In high places,
Low places,
Deep places,
Wide places.
But in my search,
I kept finding the wrong places.

In men, I searched for You.
With their kind eyes,
Flattering tongues,
And wicked hearts.

Oh, how I gave of myself.
Participating in my own defilement,
In order to find You,
But You were not there.

In success, I searched for You,

Attempting to cultivate my identity.
Finding value in what I did,
Instead of who I am,
And Whose I am.

Oh, how I received my reward.
Degrees I could hang on my wall,
Student loans and crippling debt,
Fancy job titles,
With no sense of purpose.
I had the American dream,
And You still weren't there.

In the world, I searched for You,
But quickly learned that You weren't there.
So I acquiesced to the enemy's weapons,
Instant gratification and distraction,
To sear my conscience and numb my care,
To the fact that You still weren't there.

But oh, my true Love,
It is as they say.
You leave the ninety-nine,
And go after the one who's gone astray.

In the desert, you found me,
When I was two decades plus eight.
You revealed Yourself to me,
And I knew my search had been in vain.

It was You I had been looking for.
And You had been there all along.
Standing at the door of my heart—knocking,
Waiting for me to answer,
So You could make Us a Home.

<u>MY LOVE</u>

My Father in heaven,
Words haven't been created to describe Your resplendence.
Yet, I will use the words at my disposal,
To proclaim Your glory to the world.
O Father, how great You are,
How majestic You are,
How holy You are,
How righteous You are,
How gracious You are,
How merciful You are,
How compassionate You are,
How good You are,
How sweet You are,
How gentle You are,
How forgiving You are,
How long-suffering You are,
How powerful You are,
How mighty You are.
And as for me Father,
Where do I even begin?
I am an unclean woman,
Undone by Your love for me.
How can You,
Being all that You are,

Want to love me,
Partner with me,
Be in relationship with me?
A sinner saved by grace,
Bent toward evil.
Housing places within her,
That despise You,
Rebel against You.
The very vehicle I travel through life with,
Is enmity to You.
Yet, You sent Your only, begotten Son,
To die for sins I committed.
It's not like You had other sons You could have sent.
No, You only had one,
And You sent Him to die for me.
That I may live,
And live abundantly.
O Father, I am Yours,
Now, and for all eternity.
I declare that You are my God,
And I will serve You with my life.
Where You send me Father I will go.
When You call I will answer.
I will spend the rest of my life,
Picking up my cross,
And following after You.
But O Father, I have three requests.
Will you have mercy on me?
Will you remember?
Remember that I am a sinner saved by grace.
Remember that I'm constantly at war with myself,
And sometimes I lose,
I miss the mark.

But O Father, can you remember that I am working out my salvation,
With fear and trembling?
Can you remember that the work You have started in me,
Will continue until the day of Jesus Christ?
So Father until that glorious day,
Can you help me to be who You have called me to be?

OUR LOVE

Your love is like the roar of a mighty ocean.
Your love is like the strength of a swirling wind.
Your love is like a sweet-smelling aroma,
Traveling from earth to heaven,
And then back again.
Your love calms the roar of the waves.
Your love causes the wind to cease,
Until I can hear that still small voice say,
"I in you,
You in Me,
Together our love,
Will do all things."

LISTEN

Listen to My voice,
As I guide the way.
I am your one true Love,
I will not lead you astray.

I am the One you love,
Watching over you from above.
Take My hand,
And walk with Me through this land.

The things I will show you,
If you have the faith to believe.
There is nothing I can't do,
If you keep your faith in Me.

Oh, the places we will go,
And the things your eyes will see.
To be loved,
Is a gift,
Given to you,
From Me.

RIGHTEOUS

I am calling you child,
To places your feet have never trod.
To go to My people,
To declare to them their wrongs.
There are grave sins,
That have been done before My eyes.
It is you that will warn them,
Before they meet their demise.
You are My prophet,
Whom I will send.
There is no one but you,
Who will speak My words in the very end.
They will be shocked,
Their faces in dismay,
That the Almighty God,
Still speaks,
And in this way.
Don't they know I do not change?
For I am the same,
Yesterday, forever, and today.
But you child will be unrelenting,
With the words you will speak.
You will not tickle their ears,
Or succumb to their pleas.

You will speak My words,
And detail their judgments.
Bowing before Me your God,
The One who will hold you.
They will try to harm you,
Try to silence you with threats.
But I will make your feet like deer,
So you will rise above their threats.
Together we will go,
To different nations,
And different peoples.
You will speak My words,
In order to deliver them from that which is evil.

THE RACE

I love you with an everlasting love.
There is nothing I wouldn't have done,
To build you a bridge to get you Home.

I have given My life,
So you can be set free.
Everything you need,
Can be found in Me.

I am the One who is for you.
The One who never leaves your side.
I am the One who will stand beside you,
Wrong or right.

Like a good Father,
I will rebuke and correct.
But when all is said and done,
I will never neglect.

I will be with you,
As you finish the race that must be won.
You can do it child,
I have seen it done.

THE RACE

Father You have declared and decreed,
A speaker of Your words I will be.
It's not a calling of my choosing,
But one that was given when I was born of Thee.
You have promised that You will never leave nor forsake,
But be with me with every step I take.
Like a Potter molding clay,
You are shaping me for the race.
Although I don't know what's ahead,
I have answered the call and taken Your hand.
Wherever You send me I will go,
Knowing that I'm not going alone.
Up the mountains we will climb,
Although unseen, the views will be divine.
Down the mountains we will descend,
Into the valley within.
One step after the next,
I'll make it, if I don't let go of Your hand.
Together we will cross the finish line,
Going into eternity from time.
My crown I will lay at Your feet,
And my eyes will finally see,
My Father who has always been with me.

#It is finished.

THE ENEMY OF YOUR SOUL

My brothers and sisters,
You must be made aware,
Because you are living your lives,
Like you have no cares.
Oblivious to the enemy,
And his crafty trick,
To get you to think,
That he isn't there,
And he doesn't exist.
But I'm here to warn you,
That he is alive and well,
Roaring about like a lion,
Stalking you, his prey,
Eager to pounce,
But waiting for the opportune time,
To devour.
He was created in the beginning,
To serve and worship God.
Until he succumbed to his pride,
Declaring in his heart,
That he would exalt himself above the Holy One.
A third of the angels,

He recruited in his insurrection.
But upon his failure,
He and one-third of the angels,
Fell from heaven.
In a moment, he was changed,
No longer a beautiful angel named Lucifer,
No longer an angel of light,
He became Satan,
The father of lies,
The epitome of darkness,
Void of light.
On a new quest, he embarked,
To steal, kill, and destroy,
You and me,
God's creation,
So we won't inherit eternity.
He wants us to fail,
As he did,
So he employs every wicked scheme, trick, and device,
To get us to let him in.
All he needs is an open door,
To gain a foothold,
And secure a win.
So, my brothers and sisters,
I'm writing to warn you,
Do an inventory of your life,
And shut every door that is open.
Understand that he is cunning,
Masquerading as an angel of light,
To entice you to think,
That which is wrong is right.
He loves to plant seeds,
And forge agreements,

Through your insatiable consumption,
Of entertainment and media.
Distraction,
Perversion,
Gratification,
Is what he uses to sedate you.
So that you won't choose God,
But go willingly,
To the death and destruction,
That awaits you.

DEATH AND SACRIFICE

O Father, everyone wants something for nothing,
In this microwave world of instant gratification.
Everyone wants to have it their way,
And they want it now.
They want their dreams manifested.
They speak their will into existence.
They yield to their heart's desires,
And trade the very salvation you died for them to have,
To pursue, pursue, pursue,
Obtain, obtain, obtain,
Fleshly pursuits,
Ungodly acquisitions.
And when they drink,
To the full,
The cup of their harvest,
They find it bitter,
Rancid,
Empty,
Unfulfilling.
O Father, when will the scales be removed?
When will they see,
That you didn't create them for themselves?

To be their own gods.
To go after their own way.
O Father, when will they accept the truth?
That You are the one, true living God,
Sharing Your glory with no other.
When will they turn from the world?
Lose their lives,
So they can find it.
Pick up their cross and follow You.
O, Father let them see it is only then,
They will have everything they're searching for.
Identity,
Purpose,
Love,
Life,
Peace,
Joy.
O but Father, let them be forewarned,
That they are not going to get something for nothing.
If they are going to take hold of Your gifts,
They have to take hold of You.
And the price they pay will be grave.
They will pay with their lives.
Death comes to every man,
Who chooses the living God.
Death to the old, sinful man,
That pulls them to the grave.
O Father, let them be unafraid.
Let them understand they have nothing to lose,
And everything to gain.
Freedom,
A new life,
Eternity spent with You.

SALVATION

My brothers and sisters,
I mourn for thee.
As I work out my own salvation,
With fear and trembling.
Too many of you are deceived,
Unable to see the Truth,
That will set you free.
Blind you are,
Shackled hand and feet,
Being led to your death and destruction,
Willingly.
Awake!
Hear my scream and plea.
You don't have to be captive,
In this age,
And for all eternity.
There is a Man named Jesus Christ,
Sent to earth by God,
For the sins of the world,
He was put to death and rose to life.
Because of Him,
We have been reconciled.
We are no longer slaves to sin,
Destined to die.

No, we have been liberated,
Given the gift of eternal life.
But there is a choice,
That we all must make.
Because the God of the heavens and the earth,
Doesn't force us to go His way.
So herein lies what's at stake,
Death and destruction with Lucifer, the fallen angel,
Life and freedom with GOD, our Creator.
Love,
Peace,
Rest,
Infinite blessings,
Will be your inheritance,
If you choose the One who never changes.
If your choice is to return to the One,
Who knew you before your life begun,
Say the following words aloud,
To He who will forgive you of your sins,
And become Lord & Savior of your life.
Lord, I am lost,
But I want to be found.
I am blind,
But I want to see.
I confess that I am a sinner,
And I have sinned against Thee.
But Lord will you forgive my iniquities?
Come into my heart,
And make Your home with me,
For I make You my Lord, Savior, and King,
Amen.

זה ממשיך

CONTACT THE AUTHOR

I hope you enjoyed True Love's Revelation: A Collection of Poems. If you would like to read more of my work, visit www.truelovesrevelation.com. Please also share your questions, comments, and concerns about True Love's Revelation with me at demetria_patton@truelovesrevelation.com.